A Short Guide to Research
(for designers)

MEREDITH JAMES

Marketing research seeks to sell.

Anthropology research seeks better understanding.

Design research seeks to solve, question, intervene or respond.

Introduction

Before we start looking into specific research methods, it's important to begin with an explanation on the overlaps and differences between design, anthropology and marketing. All three of these disciplines use research and can even use the same tactics. However, the function of each is quite different. These distinctions play an important role in how research is conducted. Also, there are tactics unique to design that should be given strong consideration.

This short guide gives a brief overview of different research methods employed by designers. The hope is that it will help you on your way to design wizardry.

Basic Types of Research

Research can be broken down into two main categories, quantitative and qualitative.

Quantitative: Quantitative research involves quan*tities:* numbers, amounts, percentages, measurements, and other objectively definable things. Examples include: demographics, user ratings and the results from a survey with numerical rankings.

Qualitative: Qualitative research involves qua*lities:* subjective, mutable and value-oriented. Ethnography is a good example of qualitative research.

Direct + Indirect Research

Research can also be broken down into direct
and indirect types. Direct research means you
conduct it yourself, or with a team. This is
known as primary research. While indirect
research, also known as secondary research,
is conducted by others.

Examples of primary research include: conducting
interviews, focus groups, observations and
photo-documentation. Examples of secondary
research include: research done at the library,
research conducted over the internet and case
studies written by others.

!!!! Primary research may be quantitative or
qualitative, so be careful not to confuse these
terms. (Secondary research can also be either
quantitative or qualitative.)

Information Literacy

The most commonly accessible resources for research are a (university) library and the internet. Both are secondary sources and both have access to a very large body of knowledge. The library has access to many online databases, yet the internet has an even greater abundance of information. The trick with both is to use information literacy.

What is "information literacy?" Information literacy is the term for finding and accessing quality information. It's not about how much you can find, but instead information literacy focuses on how relevant and high-quality the information is.

Being adept at finding information is a life skill that will serve you well far into the future.

University Library

Books: Colleges and universities all have libraries with a wide variety of books and materials you can check out. What you may not know is that university libraries house books that the faculty and librarians see as a benefit to students and their education. Acquisitions are made often at the request of faculty. Also, through the **Interlibrary Loan**, you can get access to books from across the country.

Articles and Journals: Through a library's website, you can also search online databases for articles in specific journals. A good but broad database aggregate is EBSCOhost. Within art and design, JSTOR is very popular.

Library Liaison: Many university libraries have a liaison dedicated to specific fields of study (like art + design). Their contact information can usually be found on the library's website. These people can be invaluable resources for finding what you're looking for.

Subject Terms

To search a library catalog or a database, there are a few things you should know. The library (like all large storehouses of information) has a structure to how it is organized. The Dewey Decimal System is an example of this. So is the Library of Congress Classification System. Regarding databases and online catalog searches, there is also an invisible structure governing the organization of information. It helps to know the difference between keywords and subject terms. When you search for keywords, the results you get can contain any of those words in any location throughout a text. Whereas subject terms are specific categories that have been assigned to a text by an actual person. Subject terms quickly give you access to all the materials on a given topic and are even sometimes listed on the inside copyright page of a book.

Find the Design and Applied Arts Index and search for articles related to graphic design.

"Graphic Design" is a set of keywords,
"Graphic Arts " is a subject term

Internet

Searching online can be overwhelming. Nowhere is information literacy more important than on the internet. Because there is a huge amount of information online, and because anyone can post things online, the vast majority of content is un-vetted / not credible. The trick with searching online is not to stop at the first search results or the easiest answer, but instead by focusing your efforts on how to find good information.

Google is simply one of several search engines, that allow users to find websites and pages (Bing, Yahoo and DuckDuckGo are others). This may surprise you, but Google has a strong influence in which websites are listed first.

To search Google properly, you must first learn about Booleans and search operators. (Please keep in mind that different search engines have different rules.)

Internet: Booleans

Booleans are named after George Boole, and they
refer to terms we use when searching to combine
or exclude categories. AND, OR and NOT are
Booleans. AND limits a search, OR broadens it,
NOT excludes one thing from the other.

CAT AND HOUSE
will return results that have both cats and
houses together.

CAT OR HOUSE
will return either cats or houses in your search
results.

CAT NOT HOUSE
will return cats except for cats affiliated with
houses.

!! Booleans also work in library databases.

Search:

site:buzzfeed.com cats AND costumes AND angry

Note how this query includes punctuation and Booleans

Compare With:

```
site:buzzfeed.com
cats AND costumes
-people -dog
```

Also note how changing your browser changes the results

Internet: Search Operators

Google uses both punctuation and search operators to help you get more accurate search results. On their site, (just Google it) you can find detailed information on both.

Some commonly used punctuation marks include the minus sign to exclude something and quote marks to search for an exact phrase:

CAT -HOUSE
returns all cats except those linked with houses

"CAT HOUSE"
returns cat houses specifically

Common search operators include:
SITE:PDX.EDU
which returns results only found on the pdx.edu website.

Internet: Web Pages

Once you've learned how to search the internet using booleans and operators, there is a second aspect to researching online: it's almost more important to be able to discern if the source you find (the page, article, blog, etc.) is of high quality.

Some examples of online content are included below, with strategies for finding quality sources among them.

Academic Journals and Publications: As is noted above, academic sources are generally high quality. Academic texts are often required to be double-blind peer-reviewed (meaning experts in the field have anonymously reviewed the materials for quality before publication). Academics are not always right, but as a general rule can be considered good sources.

Web Pages: News Sites

News Sites are a common go-to for students.
However news and media sites vary in the types
of articles they produce. Journalism is quite
different from OP/ED (opinion / editorial). There
is also a commonly understood bias to the media.
News sites don't report when things are fine.
They also can be owned by groups that have a
bias or agenda. To determine the quality of a
news report, look for its sources. Are they
conducting their own research, or just reposting
stories from the Associated Press? Also, are
their sources clearly identified on the page?
And, what are the credentials of the author?
For example, a journalist in Afghanistan will
have a direct understanding of events there,
while journalists here in New York will not.

Web Pages: Blogs

Blogs and other sites follow similar logic. The quality can vary dramatically. To find quality blogs, also seek out the credentials of the author (if a professional neurobiologist writes a neurobiology blog in his spare time, he likely knows what he's talking about). Also check the sources, are they listed on the page and are these sources substantiating claims?

I've had students suggest that they also see correlations between the quality of information on a page and the spelling, grammar and punctuation used.

Overall, the quality of information on a web page needs the same scrutiny as the search results that got you there.

Web Pages: Seek Experts

The last and final suggestion for searching online, is to seek out experts. The Museum of Modern Art is an expert in modern art. You have likely heard of them, they have been around a long time, they exist in physical space, have an address and a brick-and-mortar building.

The NOAA (National Oceanic and Atmospheric Administration) is the source for the vast majority of our weather data (you know them as the National Weather Service). They can be considered experts, just like NASA has expertise in space, astronomy and planetary imaging.

The CRAP Test

CRAP stands for Currency, Reliability, Authority, and Purpose/Point of View. The CRAP test is a way of evaluating material for its legitimacy.

Currency: Is that article or webpage current or outdated? Unless you are seeking historical information, more relevant stuff will be newer. Reliability: Is the information coming from sourced articles? Is there a reference list? Are those references also high quality? Authority: Is the information coming from an expert? Have you heard of them before? Purpose: What's the purpose of the site? If it is to sell you something, it's not credible for academia or research.

When assessing the quality of information, put it through the CRAP test. This standard is not only useful for online information, but information you find anywhere.

Secondary Sources

As books, articles, journals and online content are all coming from secondary sources, it is important to keep track of where you're getting your information from. So, please keep a list of your sources!

There are apps and sites that can help you keep track of and organize your research. Social bookmarking sites like Diigo offer these capabilities. Whatever the end result of your research (a paper, presentation, project, etc.), you are equally responsible for citing your sources, so keep them well organized and up to date... does your own work pass the CRAP test?

Find the highest quality information online about persimmons.

What is the criteria you used?

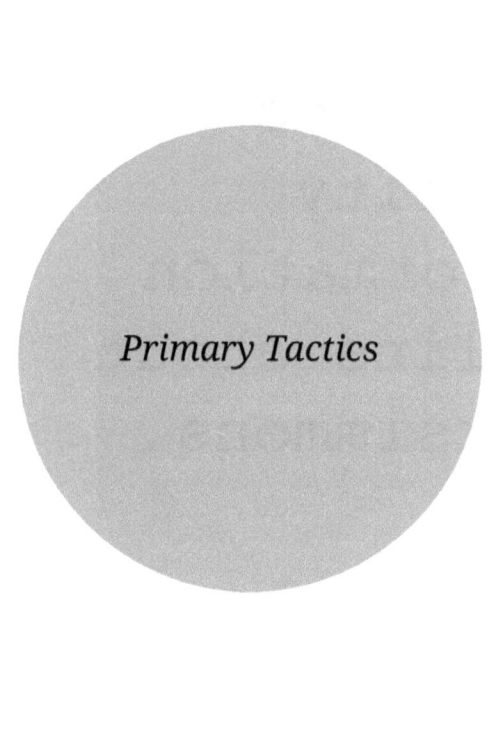

Primary Tactics

Primary Tactics

With primary research, you are the one to directly conduct the research. When doing so, it is of the utmost importance that you conduct your research ethically. Please follow the ethical guidelines set out by the American Anthropological Association.

And because primary research often involves other people, you must always ask permission when interacting directly, just as you must always allow them to change their minds. NEVER EVER force your investigations onto someone. NEVER make them feel unsafe or uncomfortable. ALWAYS be respectful. ALWAYS be honest when interacting with others. And, please keep their privacy.

As a researcher, it is equally important that you feel safe and comfortable and conduct research in public places or through legitimate organizations.

Observation

Of all the anthropological tactics, observation is the easiest, least disruptive method. If you are researching a park, go and sit in it for a few hours. Go back another day at a different time or during different weather conditions. Just sit and watch and take notes.

Observation is primary research. You are the one directly conducting the research. And because this is your own stuff, documentation is supremely important. Take careful notes, consider taking photographs or audio recordings. Notice all sensory information. Watch and listen.

Questionnaires

People also find questionnaires to be of strong benefit when conducting research. Questionnaires can ask a variety of questions, frequently with rankings or short answer boxes. Anyone can make a questionnaire online (Google Forms offers this service for free) and distribute it to your audience to fill out. Questionnaires allow your audience to choose if they want to fill them out or not.

The types of questions you ask will implicitly suggest the types of answers you receive. If you structure your questionnaire to have only yes or no answers, you will only receive yes or no responses - this will not give you insight into the *hows* or *whys*.

Interviews

Interviews are another form of primary research, one that involves direct contact with another person. Again, it is crucial you are honest and allow the person you are interviewing to stop any time they see fit.

The questions you ask in an interview are also implicit drivers of the types of answers you will get. Yes or no questions, rankings and short answer questions close a conversation down. Interviews are more intended to open conversations up. Plan four or five open-ended questions. You can always add follow-up questions on the fly. There is a big difference between asking someone, "on a scale from one to ten how much do you like your classes" (one-word answers); or asking them "do you like your classes" (short answer); and asking them, "tell me about your term so far" (open-ended).

Ethnography

Design and anthropology both use ethnographic research methods. Ethnography is intended to gain a deeper understanding of your audience, a more empathic one. Think of ethnography as a full immersion. Ethnography encompasses observations; interviews; taking photographs, videos, or documenting a place, culture or experience; letting your audience take photographs, videos or document for themselves; and a deeper awareness of the motives, thoughts, intentions, values, and beliefs of your audience.

Have you ever been a patient in the hospital? For how long? Have you thought about how overwhelming and vulnerable it feels, how much of your time is spent staring at the ceiling or how the design of the space impacts health, well-being and recovery? Ethnography seeks to understand from an *insider's* perspective.

Find a park or
a street corner
in the city
and just watch.
Notice all that
is around you.

Observation

Make a list of
the three
different types
of questions and
then ask them
of a friend.

Documenting PoV

As mentioned above, ethnography seeks a deeper understanding of a particular person, group, community, or culture and how they experience their world. You are, in a sense, seeking to best understand their point of view. As a researcher you can examine their world through photo or video or audio documentation. But you can also ask them to track their experience via their own photos, videos, audio recordings, etc.

One enlightening exercise is to have a friend go with you to the same location or event and each of you document your experience. You will each see different things, hear and notice different things and it can be an eye-opening experience to see how vastly different people experience the world around them.

Psychographics

Demographics are statistical pieces of information such as age, race, gender, height, weight and income. They are numeric and measurable (quantitative).

Psychographics however, are all of the value-based, attitudinal, preferential, subjective opinions and interests of a person or group. Which candidate in the upcoming election appeals most to you is a psychographic. If you prefer sweet foods over salty ones is another example as well as the ten most important personality traits you seek out in others.

The key to
ethnography is
to gain a deeper
understanding
and awareness
of your audience
or a particular
culture. This
is also the
foundation of
good design.

Crossover

Design, anthropology and marketing all use tactics like observations, interviews, demographics and psychographics. However, design and marketing specifically share other tactics, including:

Style and Trend Analyses
These tactics document and analyze styles and trends.

Style and Trend Projections
From analyses, projections can be made (like why and when a slick aesthetic is on the rise, or if there is a trend in hand-made / DIY goods).

Crossover

Focus Groups

When working on a project, getting a handful of people from the target audience in a room to talk with can be helpful. Focus groups are generally group discussions led by a researcher.

A / B Testing

When a designer or marketer is unsure of how the audience will respond, they may consider creating two similar but different directions (ie. one is red, the other is blue), to see which one gets the bigger response before a mass dissemination. This is called A / B Testing.

These are only a few of the more common tactics that overlap. For an expanded discussion on research tactics shared between design and marketing, please see <u>A Designer's Research Manual</u> by O'Grady and O'Grady. Please remember that a key difference between marketing, anthropology and design research is intent.

Design Tactics

Design Tools

Even though designers regularly use the tactics mentioned above, there remain tactics unique to design that often include the tools and language of design itself to better understand a place, person, group or culture.

It bears saying that designers are mediators, so design-native tactics center around the mediation / interaction of people with their ideas, information, artifacts and environments and so include research into materiality, spaces and form, not just people.

It also bears reminding that designers seek to intervene, respond or solve, so research tactics are conducted with this in mind. At multiple points in a project or process, designers will seek both insight *and* feedback from people. Early-stage research is usually secondary, while latter-stage research is usually primary.

Tactics Involving Form

Color Theory and Semiotics
Designers are trained to understand the meaning
conveyed with both color (color theory) and with
signs (semiotics). Signs can be broken up into
three categories: icon, index and symbol. Charles
Sanders Peirce goes into these categories in
detail. Designers can analyze and better
understand a certain group or culture via its
shared colors, codes and signs.

Material Affordances
In addition to color and signs, designers also
work with materials like wood, metals and
synthetics. Different materials, either in raw or
manufactured form, allow for specific affordances
(potential uses). Designers study these too.

Designers also investigate how people *respond* to
different materials. Tactility and materiality
inform haptic (touch-driven) design decisions.

Quantitative Tactics

Analytics and Metrics
It is incredibly easy to track audience behavior with digital media. Analytics and metrics are quantitative tactics that track how an audience behaves either online or through devices, products or services.

Some examples of analytics and metrics include: tracking how someone navigates a website (user flow), a user's location, their technology (hardware and software), how much time they spend doing something, counting which buttons get the most number of clicks. It is very easy to gather this data.

As a beginner, Google offers the ability to add analytics to any website (as long as you have access to the site's code). You can also view the analytics of your content on sharing sites like Twitter and Flickr.

Tactics Involving People

Another key research tactic designers employ involves people at various points in the process to understand their actions and behaviors. This is called user testing. User testing is exactly what it sounds like, users "test" out a product, idea or interface, giving the researchers (designers) feedback on how things are working or not working. Common examples of user testing include analytics and metrics, prototypes and even beta tests.

What's notable about user testing is that it can occur at multiple points in the design process. Some designers will user test an interface while others are testing functionality.

User Testing

Prototypes

Prototypes are common not only in interaction but also in product design. They aren't a research tactic per se, but rather a vehicle for helping users and designers establish a common language. Designers will create prototypes (working mock-ups) that help to elicit input and feedback. As designers are quite strong at visualizing, showing a user something tangible facilitates better discussions.

Prototypes also have the flexibility of occurring at multiple stages of the design process and with a variety of functions. A great article explaining prototypes and their various implementations was written by Stephanie Houde and Charles Hill, entitled "What do Prototypes Prototype?"

User Testing

Beta Tests

Another common type of user testing is beta-testing. Beta-tests are generally performed when everything is operational and working, but needs a final pass or two.

Famously, Gmail existing in a beta state for years. This duration is quite uncommon, but over time we've seen lots of software transition to an almost perpetual beta state with regular releases and updates.

A final note on user-testing... it's important to note that user testing comes in a variety of forms. It can be data in a spreadsheet, or live video-feed responses.

Design projects
are sometimes
thought of as
never finished,
because designers
are always
seeking further
insight and
feedback.

Raw Research

Because designers are experts at organizing and displaying information, raw research itself is treated with special care.

Two methods for organizing information include: taxonomies and mapping.

Cataloging and Taxonomies

When you gather data and begin to make sense of it, there is a process of cataloging and organizing that occurs. Groupings and hierarchies emerge.

Mapping

Maps are diagrams of an environment or network of connections. They are simply another way of organizing and displaying research.

Taxonomies and maps are *visual representations* of raw data. They also emphasize relationships among entities and larger contexts of the subject being studied.

The Form Research Takes

Visualized Research

The work of Edward Tufte showcases how raw data can be beautiful and insightful in its own way. Tufte has compiled examples from all over the world and throughout various eras and cultures of how people (designers) organize and display information.

As Tufte shows, special care is also given to *how* designers visualize raw data. We make decisions on how best to capture and display it, from drawings to photographs to numbers, marrying textual, visual and material languages most appropriate for the type of research sought. As design is creative, we also allow for a spectrum from accurate to perceptual to abstract.

Subjective Tactics

As is mentioned above, designers regularly work with subjectivity. A person's experience or response can be far from logical and instead be driven by more emotional or psychologically-oriented impulses. Note how someone's experience is shaped by mood or affect.

Perception Drawings
Ask a person or group to create a perception drawing of a space or experience.

Storytelling
Ask a person or group to tell you a story about their experience. This may or may not be interwoven with their perception of time.

One of my favorite examples comes from a student who was conducting a video interview, where her interviewee narrated stories about each memento she had in her apartment. This was an imaginative method for getting a richer perspective of a person's life.

Custom Tools

Sometimes, in order to gather the research you need, you have to create something. A prototype operates in this way, but there are additional, custom tools you can create to gather research. Custom tactics were first introduced to me by Chad Reichert, and are limited only by the imagination:

Create a scenario to see how people respond

Change the scenario to see how people respond differently.

Measure the sound- (or smell-)scape of a plaza

Incorporate aspects of time

Use thumbtacks to measure the density of different wall materials.

As designers, custom tactics can add a whole new level of awareness and meaning.

Design Archives

Conducting research also includes knowing what design ideas have existed prior. Throughout the United States (and in cities across the globe), there are archives housing artifacts and historical information on design. These institutions are amazing references and should be sought out for their knowledge of our field.

The **Cooper-Hewitt Smithsonian Design Museum** (New York) is internationally renowned for its collection.

The **Cranbrook Academy of Art Library** (Michigan) includes work from all design fields. It also houses thesis printings of every student who ever attended.

Design Archives

The **Museu del Disseny de Barcelona** (Design Museum of Barcelona) has collections spanning fashion, graphics, textiles and objects.

The Getty (Southern California) has a collection specifically focused on early twentieth century avant-garde movements like Dada and Russian Constructivism. They have also published texts on these topics.

The **Museum of Design in Zürich** (Switzerland) has an immense collection of Swiss design, with an emphasis on graphics / communication.

And of course, the **Library of Congress** is an excellent resource.

Final Thoughts

Summary

A good solid base of research involves both primary and secondary methods, along with a mix of qualitative and quantitative information. When you use multiple, yet related and directed tactics, we call this triangulation.

Most people who engage with research, start with secondary information to help shape and formulate deeper investigations, as primary research can be time-intensive and costly.

Strong research is also not random, but considered and thoughtful and follows a very clear, directed path from general to specific. The goal is not to conduct a variety of research tactics that are all disparate, the goal is to go from a broader to a deeper understanding (this is also why secondary tactics are usually conducted first).

More than anything, good research is about good listening.

Strong research, process and documentation are the foundations for creating authentic, original and contextualized work.

Further Reading

There are a variety of authors mentioned throughout the text of this short guide, but as an addition, there are a few references specific to graphic design that I will reference here (graphic design is my area of focus).

Graphic Design Thinking (Design Briefs) by Ellen Lupton and Jennifer Cole Phillips

Writing and Research for Graphic Designers: A Designer's Manual to Strategic Communication and Presentation by Steven Heller

Visual Research: An Introduction to Research Methods in Graphic Design (Required Reading Range) by Russell Bestley and Ian Noble

Colophon

This short guide originated from a series of
lectures for students on how to conduct research.
All content copyrighted Meredith James.

Running heads are typeset in Noto Serif Italic:
© 2012 Google Inc. Use through Apache license,
version 2.0.

Julius Sans One © 2012, LatinoType
(luciano@latinotype.com), use through SIL Open
Font License, 1.1.

Body text is typeset in Courier, designed by
Howard Kettler, released 1955.

Special thanks to Kris Kern and Thom Hines.

I would also like to thank the students in the
School of Art + Design at Portland State
University. Several examples contained in this
book come from them.

You are currently viewing version 1.0 of this short guide. Any examples or ideas you would like to add or have incorporated, please email the author. May, 2016.